Rubrics, Checklists & Other Assessments for the Science You Teach

By Ann Flagg

SCHOLASTIC
PROFESSIONAL BOOKS

NEW YORK • TORONTO • LONDON • AUCKLAND • SYDNEY
MEXICO CITY • NEW DELHI • HONG KONG

Rubrics, Checklists, and Other Assessments for the Science You Teach
Scholastic Professional Books, 1998

DEDICATION

To Jay Flagg for his support and encouragement over the years.

ACKNOWLEDGMENTS

Thanks to Joan Novelli for carefully crafting the manuscript into a teacher-friendly book. Thanks to every teacher who contributed student samples and ideas: Linda Hancock, Rita Devlin, Charlotte Sassman, Wendy Weiner, Jennifer Prior, Pat Sylvan, Bob Krech, Jodene Smith, Jasmine Dudzik, Terry Brock, Karen Nine, Kelly Freeman, Dee Wenner, Lynne Kepler, Debbie Weinheimer, Linda Whren, and Amy Mechling. My only regret is that we did not have room to display every sample.

Editorial Direction: Joan Novelli
Cover Design: Jaime Lucero
Interior Design: Solutions by Design, Inc.
Interior Illustration: James Graham Hale

ISBN 0-590-00486-7

Contents

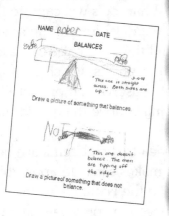

About this Book

"Today's definition of performance assessment simply formalizes a process inherent to good teaching—the process of questioning and observing students to evaluate their progress and then modifying instruction based on these observations."

— Anne Grall Reichel
"Performance Assessment: Five Practical Approaches"
Science and Children, October, 1994

Reproducibles in This Section

Teacher Checklist: Science Portfolios, page 11

Teacher Checklist: Process Skills (one for each of 8 skills), pages 12-19

Rubric Template, page 20

Einstein Attitude Check, page 21

Perhaps your memories of elementary science are like mine. I had a heavy science book that was issued on the first day of school and kept inside my desk. Once or twice each school year my class "did science" by digging out the book and reading a chapter. My teacher would supplement the reading with filmstrips and movies. The fun was over when the test was announced. I would lug my science book home and review the vocabulary words with my mother. I quickly figured out that to be good in science you had to be good at memorizing. Since that was not one of my strengths, I had surmised that I was not good at science and in fact science was no fun! It wasn't until an elementary science methods class in college that I discovered the wonder of science.

Giving children opportunities to investigate and explore the world around them is what science is all about. From hatching eggs to making models of a beaver dam, hands-on science is rewarding and worthwhile, building better observers, classifiers, and communicators, as well as encouraging curiosity. But how do you demonstrate what happens during science activities to parents, administrators, and the teacher across the hall who gives you a questioning look when you carry a pound of earthworms into your classroom? What tools will capture the scope of learning that happens in your classroom: the scientific thinking, the science attitude, and the skills children develop as they grow plants, observe metamorphosis, watch the moon, classify leaves, measure heart rates, observe and predict changes in weather, build flying things, move things with magnets, and more?

Current research supports the idea that children learn best when they are actively engaged. It makes sense to apply this thinking to assessment. According to the National Science Education Standards, assessment needs to "provide students

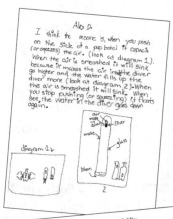

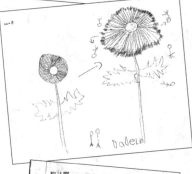

Teacher: Why do you think the grass did not grow on the natural sponges?

Alyssa: All the light was taking up the water.

Audrey: I gave it too much water....

with an opportunity to demonstrate their understanding and skill in doing science." Traditional tests tend not to be the best ways to assess what children learn, for obvious reasons. While these tests can measure knowledge of specific content, they don't capture the broader picture of what students learn as they do science: the skills they use, the attitudes they develop, the knowledge they learn outside of what a written test might cover. Performance-based assessment techniques let you assess science learning while it is happening: looking at the things children do, the questions they ask, the skills they use, and so on. Embedded in the activity in this way, assessment becomes a natural part of the learning experience. This book is designed to help you move toward active assessment. From drawings and journal entries to projects and conversations, you'll discover ways to use what's already happening in your science program as assessment tools. As you begin to bring assessment together with what children are doing in science, you'll develop a rich understanding of all that your students are learning.

Using this Book

This book is divided into four sections, each focusing on one broad category of performance assessment:

▣ **Science Writing,** page 22

▣ **Science Drawings,** page 41

▣ **Science Activities and Projects,** page 55

▣ **Science Conversations,** page 69

Along with how-tos for integrating each approach, you'll find student samples and interpretations as well as ready-to-use checklists and rubrics to guide your assessment. Tips from teachers plus a section on communicating with parents completes each section. Together these materials can help you develop assessment tools that reflect your students' growth in science: their grasp of facts and concepts, their use of process skills, and their attitudes toward science. A closer look at using each follows.

How-Tos: For each category, you'll find an explanation of why this type of assessment works (useful for sharing with parents, too). You'll also learn how to spot opportunities for weaving the particular type of assessment into your classroom activities, whether it's using write-ups of class surveys or

TEACHING TIP

Portfolio Checklist

As you gather evidence of learning—whether in the form of writings, drawings, projects, or conversations—use the checklist on page 11 to help students create well-rounded science portfolios.

recording conversations as *evidence of understanding.*

Student Samples and Teacher Interpretations: You'll meet classroom teachers from elementary schools across the country who use an inquiry-based approach to science in their classrooms. Some are just beginning to implement new assessment strategies. Others are science specialists with training. In all cases, you'll discover assessment ideas embedded in the creative and unusual science activities they share. Embedded assessment lets you observe children as they work. Checklists make it easy to look for identified areas of learning and behavior. You'll also find ideas for using pre- and post-assessments, a technique that gives you information for planning what you teach (you find out what students already know) and lets you compare growth after the lesson.

Checklists and Rubrics: Good assessment begins with identifying what you want children to learn. Whether this relates to content, skills, or attitude, there are many activities that can provide assessment information. Checklists and rubrics help guide this process. You'll find reproducible checklists and rubrics throughout the book to support your assessment efforts. Feel free to adapt any of these to best meet your needs. For more information on developing these tools, see page 9.

Sharing With Parents: These suggestions for supporting science discovery at home include reproducible Send-Home Science pages that invite parents and children to learn together.

Beginning the Evaluation Process

To begin the evaluation process, it's helpful to know that elementary science is usually divided into three broad areas: content, process skills, and attitude.

Content

Assessing content is the most common and perhaps the simplest area to assess. Scientific knowledge involves gathering information and scientific facts and developing understanding. Included in this body of knowledge are names, properties, definitions, ideas, models, and scientific "laws" and principles. The National Science Education Standards outline eight essential science content areas that all students in K-4 should understand. This book goes beyond traditional testing tools to show how you can use journal entries, drawings, interviews, and projects to draw out children's content knowledge.

- ◙ **Science as Inquiry:** Abilities necessary to do scientific inquiry—making observations, asking questions, using books and other sources of information, planning and carrying out investigations.

- ◙ **Physical Science:** Properties of objects and materials; position of motion of objects; light, heat, electricity, and magnetism.

- ◙ **Life Science:** Characteristics of organisms, life cycles of organisms, organism and environment.

- ◙ **Earth and Space Science:** Properties of earth, objects in the sky.

- ◙ **Science and Technology:** Abilities to distinguish between natural objects and objects made by humans, abilities of technological design, understanding about science and technology.

- ◙ **Science in Personal and Social Perspective:** Health, characteristics and changes in populations, types of resources, changes in environment, science and technology in local challenges.

- ◙ **History and Nature of Science:** Science as a human endeavor.

- ◙ **Unifying Concepts and Processes:** Order and organization; evidence, models, and explanation; change, constancy, and measurement; evolution and equilibrium; form and function.

Process Skills

The way scientists study the world and propose explanations derived from their work is called *inquiry*. The skills that scientists use in their investigations are called *process skills*. The National Science Education Standards define inquiry as "making observations, posing questions, examining books and other sources of information, planning investigations, reviewing what is already known in light of experimental evidence, proposing answers and explanations and communicating the results."

In the early elementary years, observation is a big part of investigation, or inquiry. As students develop science skills,

Book Link

To set up performance-based assessment stations that can "test" process skills at different age levels, see *Science Process Skills: Assessing Hands-On Student Performance* by Karen L. Ostlund (Addison-Wesley, 1992).

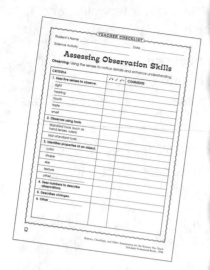

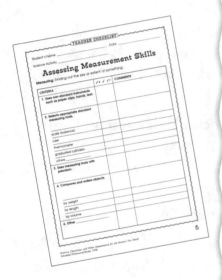

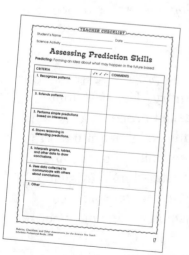

they may design and conduct simple experiments in order to answer questions. A primary goal of active science is to provide opportunities for children to use process skills and, in so doing, to build inquiry ability. Naturally, assessment of process skills involves monitoring children as they apply the skills in science activities. Process skills commonly used by kindergarten to third-grade students are:

- **Observing:** Using one or more of the five senses to gather information.

- **Classifying:** Ordering or grouping objects according to specified characteristics or systems. This skill encourages detailed observation.

- **Communication:** Exchanging information verbally, orally, or in written form.

- **Measuring:** Comparing objects to arbitrary units that may or may not be standardized.

- **Inferring:** Developing ideas based on observations and prior knowledge.

- **Predicting:** Forming an idea about what may happen in the future based on inferences.

- **Using Data:** Gathering information from observing and reading, and organizing the data in a format that others can understand, such as graphs and charts.

- **Making Models:** Developing a representation to explain an idea, object, or event.

The checklists on pages 11–21 are designed to help you assess process skills by comparing observed student performance to identified indicators. Observe children with checklists in hand to better focus on scientific behaviors that you want children to be learning. Check off those behaviors as they are exhibited by each child. You can reuse checklists during subsequent activities to note growth over time.

Science Attitude

An important goal for science instruction is the development of positive attitudes toward science. A positive science attitude includes interest, curiosity, participation, risk taking, sharing ideas, and helping others. Try the "Einstein Attitude Check" on page 21 to gather information about your students' science attitude. Before you use this assessment tool, find out what students know about Einstein. Help them understand that Einstein was one of the greatest scientists of all time. He proposed his famous theory of relativity when he was only 26. His unquenchable curiosity led him to engage in scientific investigation and delight in scientific understanding. In addition to the attitude survey, you'll gather much information intuitively as children participate in science activities. Perhaps you have noticed your students demonstrating the following positive attitudes toward science:

- is curious

- asks questions

- spends extra time and care with science investigations

- describes science as fun

- chooses books to read about science topics

- talks about science experiences from home

Resources

Active Assessment for Active Science: A Guide for Elementary School Teachers by George E. Hein and Sabra Price (Heinemann, 1995). An informative resource for teachers who want to implement authentic assessment in their science classrooms.

Doing What Scientists Do: Children Learn to Investigate Their World by Ellen Dorris (Heinemann, 1991). This book translates the theory of discovery science into a method teachers can use.

Insights & Outcomes: Assessments for Great Explorations in Math and Science by Jacqueline Barber, Lincoln Bergman, Jan M. Goodman, Kimi Hosoume, Linda Lipner, Cary Sneider, Laura Tucker (1995, Lawrence Hall of Science, University of California at Berkeley). Provides assessment for GEMS activities, but is full of suggestions that may be applied to any activity.

Making and Using Rubrics and Checklists

Assessment comes from the Latin word *assidére*, which means "to sit by as an assistant judge." As you "sit by" the students in your class to evaluate their science progress, you must decide what learning you value, what science skills you want children to develop, and what kind of attitude you want them to display toward science. The National Science Education Standards can be a starting point for understanding what children should be learning in science. (See Resources, page 10.) But it is often up to you to develop specific criteria for scoring the day to day science activities in your classroom. Rubrics and checklists simplify this process and help to ensure that you indeed evaluate what you set out to. Use the steps here to develop your own checklists and rubrics for scoring day to day science activities. A rubric template is included on page 20. For an example of a checklist format, see pages 40 and 51.

Resources, cont.

National Science Education Standards (National Academy Press; 800-624-6242; www.nas.edu). Completed in December 1995, these standards were developed with the input of thousands of individuals, including teachers, parents, curriculum developers, scientists, engineers, school administrators, and others.

National Science Resource Center. NSRC is operated by the Smithsonian Institute and the National Academy of Sciences. For information on teaching resources call (202) 786-2028.

Science and Children. The October 1994 issue is dedicated to science assessment.

A Year of Hands-on Science by Lynne Kepler (Scholastic Professional Books, 1996). Assessment strategies are included in this comprehensive and easy-to-use resource.

Step 1: Acquaint yourself with the activities.

Ask yourself:

- What are the big science concepts contained in the unit activities?

- What content do I want children to learn?

- What science skills are emphasized?

- Which scientific attitudes will children have the opportunity to display?

Step 2: Identify content, skills, and attitudes.

To assess hands-on activities you must write specific descriptions of content and skills that you expect children to learn and practice. Any one activity may contain opportunities to evaluate several areas, but it's best to focus on one or two at a time. Ask yourself these questions to identify items for evaluation:

- Of all the content to be taught, science skills to be practiced, and attitudes to be displayed in this lesson, which one or two will I evaluate?

- How can I collect evidence of learning and progress? (Throughout this book, you'll find examples of some of the many ways you can do this.)

Step 3: Create a checklist or rubric to guide assessment.

Checklists and rubrics are simple ways to organize levels of student performance. Think about what you will observe students actually doing in your classroom. Define, describe, and rank the range of behaviors or performances you can expect. This criteria for assessment lies in your own expertise as kid-watcher, and the information your curriculum or district provides about age-appropriate science behaviors. To create a checklist, simply list the expectations on a two-column chart, leaving one column for comments. To develop a rubric, record specific examples of each level on a copy of the rubric template. (See page 20.) The more specific your criteria, the easier it will be for you to score students' work. You'll find sample rubrics throughout the book.

PORTFOLIO CHECKLIST

Student's Name _____ Date _____

Science Activity _____

ITEM	DATE	ITEM	DATE
SCIENCE WRITING		**SCIENCE ACTIVITIES**	
self-evaluation of science skills		photos of children working at science stations	
rubrics		photos of science games	
written report (including rough draft)		lab report from an experiment	
cartoon strip		predictions and conclusion reached during experiment	
captions under pictures		teacher checklists to accompany science activities	
science journal entries		graphs, charts, or tables	
samples from nature notebooks		anecdotal records of process skills observed	
lab reports			
written predictions		photos of models, dioramas with rubrics to accompany the product	
science-based creative writing			
letter writing		**SCIENCE CONVERSATIONS**	
student-generated hypotheses		contributions to class concept maps	
paper and pencil tests		teacher record of child's comments while engaged in activity	
SCIENCE DRAWINGS			
pre- and post-unit drawings			
rubrics to accompany post-unit drawings		teacher notes from individual or group conferences	
paintings resulting from observations		audio tape of group discussion	
diagram with labels		transcription of child's predictions	
field journals		anecdotal records made during free exploration or science play	
pictorial report			
drawn results of experiments		student-generated questions	
maps		video tape of student presentation	
computer-generated drawings		rubric evaluation of a science drama	

Student's Name _____ Date _____

Science Activity _____

Assessing Observation Skills

Observing: Using the senses to notice details and enhance understanding.

CRITERIA	✓+ ✓ ✓−	COMMENTS
1. Uses five senses to observe.		
sight		
hearing		
touch		
taste		
smell		
2. Observes using tools.		
Standard tools (such as hand lenses, rulers)		
Non-standard tools		
3. Identifies properties of an object.		
color		
shape		
size		
texture		
other _____		
4. Uses numbers to describe observations.		
5. Describes changes.		
6. Other _____		

Rubrics, Checklists, and Other Assessments for the Science You Teach
Scholastic Professional Books, 1998

Student's Name _____ Date _____

Science Activity _____

Assessing Classification Skills

Classifying: Sorting and grouping objects according to some specified characteristics or system; encourages attention to detail and problem solving.

CRITERIA	✓+ ✓ ✓–	COMMENTS
1. **Identifies similarities and differences in properties.**		
2. **Identifies properties useful for sorting.**		
3. **Classifies objects by their properties into two groups.**		
4. **Classifies objects by their properties in multiple ways.**		
5. **Forms subgroups.**		
6. **Defines criteria and rationale for sorting.**		
7. **Other** _____		

Student's Name _____ Date _____

Science Activity _____

Assessing Communication Skills

Communicating: Exchanging information in some form such as speaking, drawing, writing, and making graphs.

CRITERIA	✓+ ✓ ✓−	COMMENTS
1. Describes object or activity accurately.		
2. Asks relevant questions.		
3. Verbalizes thinking.		
4. Discusses or orally reports on object or activity so others may understand.		
5. Constructs written reports, diagrams, drawings, graphs to communicate to others.		
6. Other _____		

Rubrics, Checklists, and Other Assessments for the Science You Teach
Scholastic Professional Books, 1998

Student's Name _____ Date _____

Science Activity _____

Assessing Measurement Skills

Measuring: Finding out the size or extent of something.

CRITERIA	✓+ ✓ ✓–	COMMENTS
1. **Uses non-standard instruments such as paper clips, hands, feet.**		
2. **Selects appropriate standard measuring tools.** scale (balance) ruler thermometer graduated cylinders others _____		
3. **Uses measuring tools with precision.**		
4. **Compares and orders objects.** by weight by length by volume		
5. **Other** _____		

Student's Name _____ Date _____

Science Activity _____

Assessing Inference Skills

Inferring: Developing ideas based on observations and prior knowledge.

CRITERIA	✓+ ✓ ✓–	COMMENTS
1. **Uses all appropriate information in making inferences.**		
2. **Separates appropriate from non-essential information.**		
3. **Develops ideas (inferences) based on observations.**		
4. **Develops ideas based on prior knowledge.**		
5. **Shows sound reasoning in defending inferences.**		
6. **Interprets graphs, tables, and other data to support inferences.**		
7. **Other _____**		

Rubrics, Checklists, and Other Assessments for the Science You Teach
Scholastic Professional Books, 1998

Student's Name _____ Date _____

Science Activity _____

Assessing Prediction Skills

Predicting: Forming an idea about what may happen in the future based on inferences.

CRITERIA	✓+ ✓ ✓−	COMMENTS
1. Recognizes patterns.		
2. Extends patterns.		
3. Performs simple predictions based on inferences.		
4. Shows reasoning in defending predictions.		
5. Interprets graphs, tables, and other data to draw conclusions.		
6. Uses data collected to communicate with others about conclusions.		
7. Other _____		

Student's Name _____ Date _____

Science Activity _____

Assessing Data Collection Skills

Collecting Data: Gathering information from a variety of sources including observing, questioning, and reading.

CRITERIA	✓+ ✓ ✓–	COMMENTS
1. Decides how to efficiently gather data.		
2. Gathers necessary data correctly.		
3. Records data correctly.		
4. Organizes data collected.		
into charts		
into graphs		
into content webs		
other _____		
5. Makes statements in own words about data gathered.		
6. Applies data to new ideas.		
7. Other _____ _____		

Rubrics, Checklists, and Other Assessments for the Science You Teach
Scholastic Professional Books, 1998

Student's Name _____ Date _____

Science Activity _____

Assessing Model-Making Skills

Making Models: Making representation of objects with different materials.

CRITERIA	✓+ ✓ ✓−	COMMENTS
1. Understands how models can represent objects, ideas, or events.		
2. Explains similarities and differences between a model and the real thing.		
3. Uses pre-made model to communicate information.		
4. Develops own appropriate model to represent an object, idea, or event.		
5. Uses own model to communicate learning or ideas.		
6. Other _____		

Student's Name _____ Date _____

Science Topic _____

SCORE	CRITERIA	COMMENTS
3	**Capable**	
2	**Developing**	
1	**Beginning**	

Rubrics, Checklists, and Other Assessments for the Science You Teach
Scholastic Professional Books, 1998

Name _____ Date _____

Einstein Attitude Check

Directions: Read each sentence and color the picture that best describes how you feel about the statement.

Color one.

1. Science is fun and interesting.

2. I would like to be put in charge of a science project for our class.

3. I wish we had more time to do science activities at school.

4. I like to watch science on T.V.

5. I like to read books about science.

6. Scientists have an interesting job.

7. I am good at science.

Use the back of this paper to tell more about how you feel about science.

Using Writing for Assessment

You'll want to be sure to include opportunities for both new and experienced writers among your science assessment strategies. Science motivates beginning writers to use emerging skills to record their findings. Science stories, notebooks, journals, lab sheets, written tests, and other written forms of assessment are rich sources of information. Very young children are less likely to demonstrate all that they are thinking through the written word. One way to overcome the writing barrier is to encourage children to accompany writing with non-verbal forms of communication such as drawings and graphs. Writings coupled with teacher conferences can reveal more, too. Checklists and rubrics will help you and your students glean assessment information from writing.

Why Writing Works

Using children's writing as an assessment tool fits in naturally with science and the primary classroom.

- Science notebooks provide a structure for guiding children's writing and scientific thinking.

- Science journals serve as a vehicle for written dialogue between teacher and student.

- Writing or dictating science-based stories requires students to combine written communication skills, science knowledge, and creativity.

- Science journals provide a way for students to record observations over time.

- Teacher-created short answer tests can parallel hands-on investigations and provide tangible feedback.

- Paper and pencil tests can be an effective way to measure growth when content learning is the goal.

- Children learn to reflect on what they understand through written science journals.

- Science writing teaches the process of communicating like real scientists by providing opportunities for children to describe procedures, record observations, and report conclusions in science logs.

- Attitudes can show through in children's writing.

- Some children are more comfortable sharing their thoughts in writing than they are sharing them aloud.

Evaluating Science Writing

Writing can contain evidence of emerging process skills and insight into children's way of thinking. What should you look for when you read a child's science writing? Use this checklist as a guide.

1. Look for evidence of process skills.

   Example: Amanda correctly recorded the exact height of her bean plant.

2. Look for accurate facts and other information.

   Example: John drew a picture of three mammals and wrote the names of each.

3. Evaluate writing based on a pre-established set of criteria.

   Example: An exemplary journal entry will:

   - contain a description of the appearance of the moon on at least 15 nights,

   - correctly label the name of the phase observed,

   - identify the moon as either waxing or waning,

   - explain how the moon has changed over time.

4. Evaluate writing holistically. Look for signs that the student has internalized a concept.

   Example: After being certain that magnets were attracted to all kinds of metal, Jorgé wrote in his journal that magnets would not attract a penny.

5. Evaluate writing looking for clues about scientific attitudes.

To help children reflect on what they've learned, I have them write in science "thinking journals." I ask a specific question about what we are learning and give students time to respond.

Karen Nine
Desert Vista Elementary School
Apache Junction, Arizona

Example: Joan is eager to write in her journal after she observes the hamster.

6. Look for growth over time in children as observers and recorders of information.

Example: Jay accurately drew and labeled six snails on his lab sheet this week. Last week he only recorded observations of one snail.

7. Notice use of language arts skills in science writing.

Example: Royce included adjectives in his written description of the windowsill garden.

Using Rubrics and Checklists to Assess Writing

Rubrics let you assess student performance based on specific criteria. You can copy and use the rubric on page 38 to get an overall picture of a child's science writing. Share the rubric with students before the task to help them set goals for themselves. Use the same rubric to assess a variety of writing tasks over time. Compare early scores to later scores to show growth and to help students continue to set learning goals.

Rubrics can help you communicate with parents as well. Have them handy at conference time, along with students' samples, to help parents understand where their children are and what they are moving toward. Additional rubrics to use with students' writing appear at the end of this section on pages 35–40. Remember to plug in the reproducible process skill checklists on pages 11–20 as they apply, too.

SELF-ASSESSMENT

Name _____ Date _____
Journal Entry Topic _____

Science Vocabulary and Facts

Check the boxes that tell about your journal entry.

	A Lot	Some	A Little
1. I include facts in my journal. In this entry, I counted ____ facts.			
2. I use new science vocabulary. Some of the words I used are: _____			
3. I used what I already knew to help explain what I learned. Something about this topic I already knew is: _____			

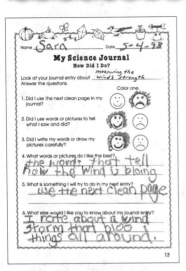

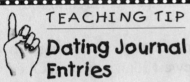

TEACHING TIP

Dating Journal Entries

Encourage students to date journal entries just as real scientists do. This makes it easy to return to entries over time to note growth. Rather than bog down very young children by requiring that they write the date on each page, provide a date stamp from an office supply store.

Closeup on Science Journals

Journals used in conjunction with science can take on different forms and be used for a variety of purposes. However you choose to use journals in your classroom, you can use the rubric on page 38, as well as the self-assessment form on page 37, to evaluate students' entries.

◉ Journals can serve as a science log and be evaluated as a final product. Children describe experimental procedures, record observations, and report conclusions. Children who keep science logs learn to attend to detail and write observations. The log serves as a record of science in progress. You can use the conclusions children record as a final report on a scientific investigation and a way to assess scientific knowledge.

◉ Journals can be formative and serve as a window into a child's thinking. Unlike science logs, the formative journal is not an end product but a tool that facilitates thinking as students move toward a final product or work through investigations contained in a unit. Formative journal entries reveal the process involved in forming concepts.

Traditional With a Twist

With all this talk about hands-on evaluation you may be reluctant to administer a traditional paper and pencil test. But written tests can be an effective way to measure growth when content learning is the goal. Whether you write your own tests or use one from the textbook, look over these suggestions to see if your test makes the grade.

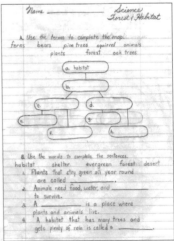

◉ Does your test feature problems that require more than one step to reach a solution?

Example: How is a toad the same as a frog? How is it different?

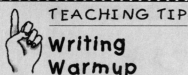
Writing Warmup

Before I ask children to write, I often provide samples to encourage students and provide an informal guideline for writing. When children see the writing of other students their age, they realize that my expectations and their writing abilities can connect. Sometimes I reproduce anonymous samples from last year's class onto overhead transparencies. As we critique the samples, I ask questions like: "What do you like about this sample?" "How could this writing improve?" "Is there something in this sample that you would like to try?" After a warmup like this my class is eager to write and show me what they can do.

Ann Flagg
Edu-Prize School
Gilbert, Arizona

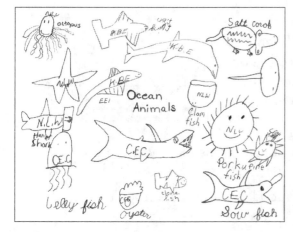

◎ Does your test leave room for creative thinking or more than one possible answer?

Example: Draw a plant that can survive in a dry climate and label its features.

◎ Does your test require that students apply data or concepts generated earlier in hands-on investigations?

Example: Circle the foil shape that will float.

◎ Does your test parallel hands-on investigations?

Example: The test may use a picture of an investigation that the children encountered in class.

Example: What may have happened to this wilted bean plant?

◎ Does your test provide opportunities for children to estimate or predict?

Example: Arrange the glasses containing colored water in order from the highest to the lowest sound you think they will make.

◎ Does your test provide opportunities for original questions, plans, graphs, or charts?

Example: Design a container that will protect an egg from a 6-foot fall.

Shared Science Writing

Self-assessment happens naturally and science concepts are enlarged when students share ideas through science writing. By looking over a few shoulders you can pick out opportunities for assessment, too. Starter ideas follow.

Science-Go-Round: Make science writing a game. Seat children in groups of three for a pre-unit brainstorming session. Introduce a topic like Ocean Animals and have one child write the topic in the center of the page. Have the first child write a word (or draw a picture) associated with oceans on the paper, initial her contribution, and pass the paper to the child on her right. The second child writes an ocean animal, initials it, and passes the paper to the child on his right. The activity continues until no one in the group can record another word. (You may allow children to pass if they can't think of a word, or ask a neighbor for help.) Collect the papers and note the initials to get insight into prior knowledge. Try the game again

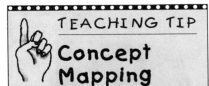
TEACHING TIP
Concept Mapping

Setting up concept mapping on your computer is a snap with *Inspiration*, software designed for mapping, webbing, outlining, and organizing. A book of classroom ideas for and by teachers is available as well. This software was only $19.95 when we checked. Call Inspiration Software at (800) 877-4292 for more information.

at the end of the unit and collect the papers for an excellent pre- and post-assessment comparison.

One Scientist to Another: Divide your class into two groups. Give one group a simple investigation to complete— for example, given a collection of materials, devise a way to test which ones are attracted to a magnet. Next, have each child who completed the investigation explain the process in writing, including materials needed and steps to follow. Have these children share the procedure for the investigation with classmates who have not yet participated. (These will be the children in the second group.) Provide materials. Can the second child recreate the activity accurately? Self-assessment for both groups will happen naturally as Group 2 tries the investigation.

Pair and Share: After a science experience, ask children to articulate their thoughts in journal form. Pair up students to read their entries to one another for a new point of view. Exchange science journals on a regular basis to keep feedback flowing.

Round-Robin Writing: Set the stage by featuring a topic, activity, or question that originates in a science unit students are studying. Give one child a piece of paper to record theories or thoughts about the topic. Pass the paper around so that each child can read the comments and record a contribution. Ideas come together as classmates share with one another.

Community Concept Maps: Together, create a primary concept map to unpack science topics. A pre-, mid-, and post-concept map helps keep ideas developing. Follow these steps to make concept maps:

1. Write a key concept at the top of a sheet of chart paper or oaktag.

2. Add linking words.

3. Brainstorm sub-concepts that relate to key concepts.

4. Add linking words.

5. Add information about subconcepts.

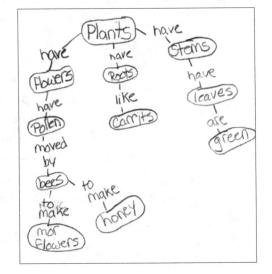

Assessment in Action

The following student samples offer an inside look at some of the ways teachers are using writing to assess content, process skills, and attitudes. You'll see that although journals are a wonderful way to assess learning, there are many other creative ways to weave this technique into your science program. Examples of children's work are followed by comments from their teachers. When using similar assessments in your classroom, you'll bring your own knowledge of each student to the evaluations. Look for tips in the margins of these pages for additional help in implementing these assessment strategies in your classroom. The reproducible checklists and rubrics on pages 35–40 will provide additional support.

Evaluating Content
Student-Generated Quizzes

When Jasmine Dudzik's students study earth science, they sign up for topics that interest them. To demonstrate their understanding, children divide up into groups to prepare a report and class presentation on the topic of their choice. As part of the presentation, students must devise an assessment to administer to the class. They get very creative with the assessment. Jasmine has had students present assessments in the form of games, team quizzes, and panel discussions. The one included here is a student-generated quiz.

Objective: Students will demonstrate an understanding of volcanoes by completing a student-generated assessment.

Assessment: The team devised a set of thoughtful questions. The questions represent most of the volcano topics we covered. I appreciate that they included answers with the test. Answers demonstrate the "testers'" understanding of the subject.

Jasmine Dudzik
Pleasant Ridge School
Saline, Michigan

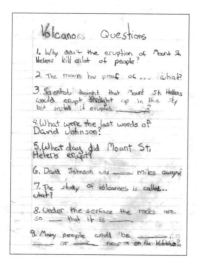

Too much pressure builds up so the volcano has to erupt.

TEACHING TIP
Managing Teamwork

Most students enjoy working in pairs or in a team of three. To facilitate collaboration, we discuss teamwork skills at the onset of the school year. Presenting their own assessments to the class seems to boost students' self confidence and sense of empowerment, in addition to helping them retain subject content due to their high sense of ownership.

Jasmine Dudzik
Pleasant Ridge Elementary
Saline, Michigan

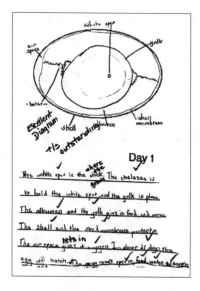

Letters and Literature

After her third-grade students plant seeds in cups and carefully tend them, Lynne Kepler assesses what they've learned about plants by having the children respond to literature. She reads "The Garden" from *Frog and Toad Together* by Arnold Lobel (HarperCollins, 1972). In the story Toad tries a variety of funny techniques to get his flowers to grow. After reading the story she has students write letters to Toad explaining what is really necessary for a garden to grow. You can adapt this idea to use with other literature, both fiction and nonfiction. For example, with Eric Carle's classic story, *Papa, Please Get the Moon For Me* (Picture Book Studio, 1986), stop reading before the end of the book and have children write their own ending that explains what happened to the moon after it disappeared.

Objective: Students will include the sequence and important elements of plant growth (water, sun, air, soil, warmth) in a letter to Toad.

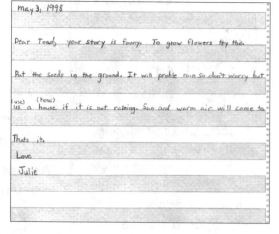

Assessment: Julie included most of the important elements needed for plants to grow in her letter. The humor she included was fun, too, and showed her positive attitude toward science.

Lynne Kepler
Clarion Limestone School
Strattanville, Pennsylvania

Scoring Science Notebooks

When Pat Sylvan's second-grade students hatched chickens in the classroom, they kept science notebooks to record changes from the time the eggs were placed in the incubator to hatching day. They used resources to learn more about what was happening inside the eggs. To encourage students to record detailed information, Pat designed a system to assess use of vocabulary and information included. Each science word and fact or observation gets a check. Pat adds them up to assign a grade. You can have students use the self-assessment checklist on page 39 to assess their own use of vocabulary and facts.

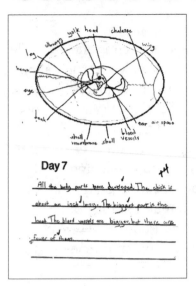

Day 7

All the body parts have developed. The chick is about an inch long. The biggest part is the head. The blood vessels are bigger, but there are fewer of them.

Objective: Students will combine research and observations to write a detailed log describing a chick's development.

Assessment: Jacqueline did an exceptional job of drawing, labeling, and recording changes in the egg. Each time she used science vocabulary to accurately record a fact I gave her one check. I can compare the number of checks from one journal entry to the next to see evidence of growth in science vocabulary and content. This system also helps children set goals for themselves and allows parents to easily follow their children's progress at conference time.

> Pat Sylvan
> Pine Grove Elementary School
> Simsbury, Connecticut

Pre- and Post-Unit Writing

As part of a nine-week Plant Nursery unit, Kelly Freeman's students learned about plant life and ecology. They built terrariums, tried basic grafting, and represented the water cycle with models and demonstrations. To wrap up the unit, they wrote and illustrated nonfiction stories about plants.

Objective: Students will organize factual information about plants into well thought out pieces of nonfiction writing.

Assessment: Devyn did a great job comparing root systems. She writes about how plants defend themselves and even tries to explain photosynthesis. However, Devyn neglected to pull in several key concepts about plant parts, a major focus of the science lesson. She showed me that she did some additional research by mentioning the Lucille Ball Rose. Her interest in learning more is one of the ways Devyn demonstrates a positive attitude about the topic and science in general. I will challenge Devyn to pull in more of the information she learns in her writing when we write about our next science topic.

> Kelly Freeman
> Edu-Prize School
> Gilbert, Arizona

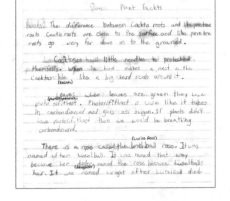

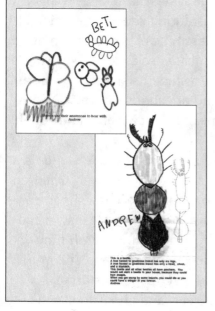
Writing to Evaluate Process Skills

How Things Work

Cartesian diver systems are engaging science inquiry activities for children. Jasmine Dudzik shows her students a system she has made and demonstrates how it works. Then she asks them to construct their own, without written directions or adult assistance. Students observe their closed systems carefully and then explain in writing how they think the divers float and sink.

Objective: The student will explain what makes a Cartesian diver float and sink.

Assessment: Alex has made the connection between the bottle being squeezed and the diver sinking. He noticed that when pressure is put on the sides of the bottle, the water level inside the eye dropper goes up. This shows that Alex is a careful observer. He also infers that the increase in water inside the dropper causes it to sink. At this level I do not expect students to fully understand the principles of buoyancy and density behind the Cartesian diver, but I was pleased to see that careful observation and inference had revealed some of the mechanics behind what causes something to sink or float.

Jasmine Dudzik
Pleasant Ridge Elementary
Saline, Michigan

What Do You Think?

Young children make predictions all the time: Do those clouds mean it's going to storm? Will the caterpillar turn into a moth or a butterfly? Can a magnet pick up everything that's metal? How tall will this plant grow? Charlotte Sassman frequently asks her students to write down predictions related to science questions before sharing them with their classmates. This gives each child a chance to formulate an idea independently of other children, especially important for children who may not feel comfortable speaking up or who need a little extra time to think.

The sample that follows shows how Charlotte used this technique in her class. After an investigation of the properties of

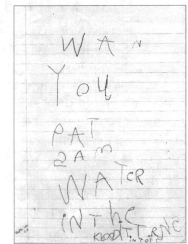
water, which included using an eyedropper to put water on a hot skillet, watching ice melt, and catching water vapor on a cookie tray, she asked children to predict what would happen if they set a pan of water outside on a very cold day. Instead of sharing ideas aloud, students recorded their predictions in their journals.

Objective: To predict what will happen to water that is exposed to freezing temperatures.

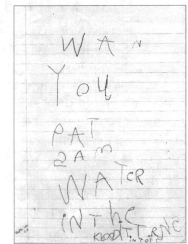

Assessment: Paul's prediction, "wan you pat sam water in the klood it trns in to iis" (when you put some water in the cold it turns into ice) shows me that he understands how to make a prediction. Paul also understands the science concepts contained in the unit and knows that the print he put on the page is meaningful. When he read this passage out loud to me, he was seeing himself as a reader. Not all of the words are spelled correctly, but he confidently writes his science idea on paper.

> *Charlotte Sassman*
> *Alice Carlson Applied Learning Center*
> *Fort Worth, Texas*

Attitude and Interest

You'll see many signs of your students' attitudes toward science as they engage in various activities throughout the day. Do they look forward to science activities? Is science a favorite subject? Do students ask questions during science investigations? Take part? Offer to help classmates? Share information? Do their everyday conversations include science? If you have a class aquarium, plants, or a pet, do students spend free time observing? In addition to recording anecdotal information, you can assess this important element of science learning through children's writing.

For example, Karen Nine asks her second-grade students a question that requires more than a yes or no answer. Children have time to journal predictions or thoughts. Then she introduces an activity or reading that can help them to answer the question. Students "take notes" by listing information they've learned. Finally, Karen asks the question again and children write informed responses. Within these responses are clues about children's interest in the subject, and about their atti-

Book Link

The Rookie-Read-About-Science series is a terrific place to turn for easy-to-understand explanations to children's science questions. *Solid, Liquid, Gas* by Alan Fowler (Children's Press, 1995) gives a simple explanation about the states of water.

TEACHING TIP

Up-Close Observations

If you expect children to observe closely, it is sometimes best to give each child his own set of equipment. In the example on page 31, children were given their own Cartesian Diving Systems to manipulate and observe, allowing them to work at their own pace and get close enough to the materials to make careful observations.

Jasmine Dudzik
Pleasant Ridge Elementary
Saline, Michigan

tudes toward science in general. The sample here shows some of the signs to look for.

Objective: Students will be able to explain how fish breathe under water, and will demonstrate enthusiasm and curiosity about the science topic.

Assessment: To better understand Ally's journal entry, I sat down to conference with her. I was pleased to see that Ally included a description of how fish breathe. The extra information Ally added about the fish's swim bladder showed me her enthusiasm and interest in the subject. Our conversation, transcribed below, also captures Ally's curiosity.

Teacher: What was the most important fact that you learned today?

Ally: I learned two neat things. Fish can drown in air. They have bladders that blow up.

T: Why do fish have swim bladders?

Ally: So they won't sink. So they can float.

T: If you were a fish, how would you catch a yummy little fish to eat at the bottom of the ocean?

Ally: I'd swim for it.

T: Yes, but how would you go down in the water?

Ally: I'd take air out of my bladder so I'd sink down near the yummy fish.

T: You wrote that fish don't drown because there is oxygen under the water. Tell me more.

Ally: They breathe from gills.

T: How?

Ally: They open and close and fish take oxygen from the water.

T: Why do fish drown in air?

Ally: They can't breathe in air like we can't breathe in water

T: Good! What would you like to learn about next?

Ally: I was wondering what the inside of coral are made of.

Karen Nine
Desert Vista School
Apache Junction, Arizona

Watch Them Grow

Comparing baseline information with later observations from children is an effective way to demonstrate growth to parents. On the first or second week of school I ask the children two questions: "What is science?" and "What have you done in science that makes you feel good about yourself?" I record children's exact words on a form that I place in their science folders. At the end of the year, I ask the same two questions, again recording their answers. We compare the two sets of responses to see growth. Their early answers often reflect "TV science," mostly from Bill Nye! By the end of the year, the children always know what scientists do and have a good self concept about themselves as scientists.

Charlotte Sassmann
Alice Carlson Applied
Learning Center
Fort Worth, Texas

Sharing with Parents

If you are just beginning to implement alternative assessment techniques, it may be challenging at first to communicate with parents about the validity of some of your assessment tools. Parents need to be reassured that your new methods are as good or better than traditional test scores. Set the stage by sending home a letter like the one shown; then, on conference day, work with these practical suggestions.

- Be confident that your alternative testing gives reliable evidence of science learning.

- Keep it simple. Don't overwhelm parents with too many details behind the process.

- Explain your criteria and how each sample gives evidence of objectives met or objectives not yet attained.

- Partner with parents. Often they can share insights that will enrich your understanding of the child.

- Start with a balanced approach. If your school has been using a traditional approach to assessment, introduce new techniques along with the old. As the year progresses and everyone becomes more comfortable with your new assessment tools, include more and more samples in the portfolios.

- Leave time for questions. Listen to parent concerns and respond as someone who is learning and striving to improve.

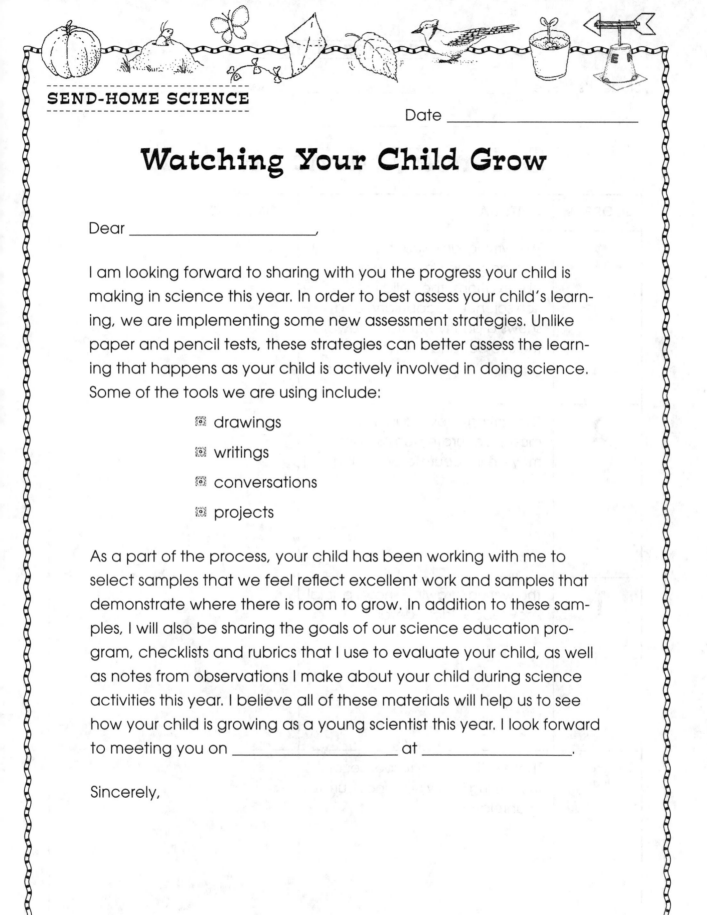

Date _____

Watching Your Child Grow

Dear _____,

I am looking forward to sharing with you the progress your child is making in science this year. In order to best assess your child's learning, we are implementing some new assessment strategies. Unlike paper and pencil tests, these strategies can better assess the learning that happens as your child is actively involved in doing science. Some of the tools we are using include:

- drawings
- writings
- conversations
- projects

As a part of the process, your child has been working with me to select samples that we feel reflect excellent work and samples that demonstrate where there is room to grow. In addition to these samples, I will also be sharing the goals of our science education program, checklists and rubrics that I use to evaluate your child, as well as notes from observations I make about your child during science activities this year. I believe all of these materials will help us to see how your child is growing as a young scientist this year. I look forward to meeting you on _____ at _____.

Sincerely,

Student's Name _____ Date _____

Activity_____

Science Journal Rubric

SCORE	CRITERIA	COMMENTS
3	The writing/drawing shows detail and accuracy in recording observations; the child uses rich science vocabulary, and shows a positive attitude toward the subject and science in general.	
2	The writing/drawing includes mostly accurate details; some may be inaccurate or missing.	
1	The writing/drawing shows partial knowledge; lacks detail.	
0	There is little or no response, or the writing/drawing is inaccurate or unrelated.	

Rubrics, Checklists, and Other Assessments for the Science You Teach
Scholastic Professional Books, 1998

Name _____ Date _____

My Science Journal
How Did I Do?

Look at your journal entry about _____ .
Answer the questions.

Color one.

1. Did I use the next clean page in my journal?

2. Did I use words or pictures to tell what I saw and did?

3. Did I write my words or draw my pictures carefully?

4. What words or pictures do I like the best?

_____

_____

5. What is something I will try to do in my next entry?

_____

_____

6. What else would I like you to know about my journal entry?

_____

_____

_____

Student's Name _____ Date _____

Activity _____

Assessing Science Writing

SCORE	CRITERIA	COMMENTS
3	**EXEMPLARY**	
	thorough understanding of concepts	
	frequent application of science learning	
	excellent detail in observation	
	completion of all tasks	
	superior communication skills	
	outstanding evidence of creative thinking	
2	**PROFICIENT**	
	solid understanding of concepts	
	regular application of science learning	
	detailed observations	
	completion of most tasks	
	good communication skills	
	evidence of creative thinking	
1	**PROGRESSING**	
	some understanding of concepts	
	occasional application of science learning	
	adequate observations	
	completion of some tasks	
	communicates with prompting	
	learning to be a creative thinker	

Rubrics, Checklists, and Other Assessments for the Science You Teach
Scholastic Professional Books, 1998

Name _____ Date _____

Journal Entry Topic _____

Science Vocabulary and Facts

Check the boxes that tell about your journal entry.

	A Lot	Some	A Little
1. I include facts in my journal. In this entry, I counted _____ facts.			
2. I use new science vocabulary. Some of the words I used are: _____ _____ _____			
3. I used what I already knew to help explain what I learned. Something about this topic I already knew is: _____ _____ _____ _____			

Name _____   Date _____

Topic _____

Science Skills

Read each statement. Check the boxes to tell about your science journal.

	I Did Great!	I Did Okay	I Need to Work on This
1. I described what I saw.			
2. I used accurate and careful details.			
3. I described similarities or differences.			
4. I used pictures to help tell what I saw.			
5. I labeled my pictures.			
6. I used the information I collected to draw a conclusion.			

Rubrics, Checklists, and Other Assessments for the Science You Teach
Scholastic Professional Books, 1998

Using Drawings for Assessment

TEACHING TIP

What the Standards Say

Using drawings as an assessment tool supports guidelines set forth by the National Science Education Standards, which state that "assessment tasks must be developmentally appropriate, must be set in contexts that are familiar to the students, must not require reading skills or vocabulary that are inappropriate to the students grade level, and must be as free from bias as possible."

Effective science assessment can be as simple as spreading out the colored pencils and providing blank paper for your eager young scientists to draw and record observations, understandings, and more. With a watchful eye and thoughtful preparation, these drawings can provide tangible evidence of students' progress.

Why Use Drawings?

Using drawing as an assessment technique fits naturally with science and the primary classroom. Here's how.

- Drawing comes naturally to children, who from an early age use this art form as a means to express their thoughts.

- Children often relax as they sketch, allowing what they know to flow on the paper.

- Pre-writers, non-English-speaking students, and children who are uncomfortable with the writing process can all communicate through drawing.

- Drawings are positive. They draw out what the child understands, rather than point out what the child doesn't know.

- Drawings are a natural extension of hands-on activities, making it easy to incorporate evaluation right into a lesson.

- Drawings make great conversation starters, allowing you to learn more about what a child knows, and at the same time eliminating the "I don't know" responses that can occur with oral questioning or writing alone.

- Drawings offer students feedback on their own learning. Students can literally see their learning progress and are encouraged.

- Drawings offer you feedback, too. Use the information gleaned from drawing assessment to steer the direction of the unit.

Encouraging Creativity

Drawings let young children demonstrate some of what they know, in ways they might not be able to express with words. When you use drawings as an assessment tool, keep developmental considerations in mind. Some children may be more adept with pencils and crayons than others. "Messy" drawings may actually represent a child's best work. More tips for encouraging students' efforts follow.

- ⚙ Provide a climate for creative expression that allows for divergent thinking. (Don't expect children to draw what they see the same way.)

- ⚙ Let students compare drawings to see the many ways of looking at something.

- ⚙ Look for assessment information in the drawing process, not just in the product.

Using Rubrics and Checklists to Assess Drawings

With science drawings, as with any artwork, the process has as much to tell as the end product. What can you learn by observing the way children approach their science work? Turn casual observations into meaningful assessment by looking for specific, desired behaviors that point to active learning. Use the checklists and rubrics on pages 50–53 (or your own versions) to guide your observations.

Remember to use the reproducible process skills checklists on pages 11–20 to support assessment of drawings, too. Share these assessment tools with students to help them set goals for themselves. You can use one rubric to assess a variety of drawings over time to show growth and to help students continue to set learning goals. Use the rubrics and checklists to communicate with parents as well. Have them handy at conference time, along with students' drawings, to help parents understand what their children have learned and what goals they might set.

TEACHER CHECKLIST

Student's Name _____ Date _____
Science Activity _____

The Drawing Process

Customize this checklist by filling in the blanks with the subject of the student's drawing.

	EXEMPLARY	DEVELOPING	BEGINNING
Shows an interest in _____ even before it is formally introduced.			
Returns to observe _____ on a daily basis.			
Adds to the drawings in the journal without being reminded.			
Stops frequently to observe when making drawings.			
Discusses observations with other students.			
Uses science vocabulary during observation and drawing sessions.			
Demonstrates a growing curiosity by asking questions.			
Applies prior knowledge in thinking about _____ and planning drawings.			
Utilizes a variety of tools (rulers, colored pencils) in observing.			
Notices and records changes in _____ over time.			

Rubrics, Checklists, and Other Assessments for the Science You Teach
Scholastic Professional Books, 1998   51

TEACHER CHECKLIST

Activity _____

Class Record: Assessing Drawings

✓+ exemplary
✓ proficient
✓– needs improvement
– not evident

NAMES

Rubrics, Checklists, and Other Assessments for the Science You Teach
Scholastic Professional Books, 1998   53

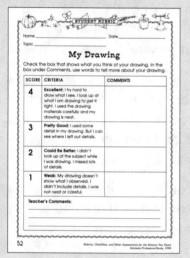
9 Steps to Assessing Drawings

Keep these guidelines in mind as you look for evidence of learning in drawings.

1. What is your first impression of the work? Is it rushed and careless or neat and accurate? Scientific attitude and desire to share findings can come across in the quality of the work.

2. Has the student taken the time to include labels, speech bubbles, or sentences that elaborate on the drawings? Look for evidence of new vocabulary and an understanding of concepts or facts.

3. Are the drawings stereotypic or realistic? Realism can demonstrate that the child gathered information through observation or by completing an experiment.

4. Consider spelling and handwriting, but concentrate primarily on the science content of the work.

5. Jot down the objectives or criteria of the lesson and keep them near you as you evaluate the drawings. Search for evidence in the drawings that the children have met the criteria.

6. Look beyond the minimum criteria and expect to pull out strengths and knowledge that the child brings to the project. Drawing is an avenue through which students can demonstrate scientific understanding beyond the established criteria.

7. Collect more than one drawing—or use another kind of assessment on similar topics—to validate or clarify student understanding.

8. Compare drawings from the beginning of the unit with drawings done at the end. Look for evidence of learning and share it with the student.

9. Meet with the student as soon as possible and evaluate the work together. Children will often share insightful comments that will enhance your understanding.

Helping Children Make the Most of Drawings

"I'm finished!" If cries like this bring students' drawings to a premature stop, try some of these practical tips:

- ◎ Share field guides and illustrated science books with children. Compare live plants or animals with the professional pictures found in the books. Work with the children to define what makes a useful scientific drawing.

- ◎ Have each child share his drawing with the class. Encourage honest comments. Ask children who include accurate detail to share the intricacies of their work. If the drawing is sparse, offer comments on what is there rather than what is not there, and then privately challenge the child to extend his work.

- ◎ Post appropriate scientific posters around the room for inspiration. Animal and plant posters are often available at no charge from local wildlife or land management government agencies.

- ◎ Plan to do a series of drawings on the same subject. Encourage children to evaluate their own work and to attempt to improve with each successive drawing.

Assessment in Action

The following samples offer an inside look at some of the ways teachers are using drawings and diagrams to evaluate content, process skills, and attitude in their classrooms. Use the samples to guide your own assessment efforts as you look at students' drawings, keeping in mind that you will bring your own knowledge of your students to the process. Look for practical tips in the margins. Checklists and rubrics at the end of this section will further support your assessment efforts.

Drawings to Evaluate Content

What Do You See?

In the spring, Terry Brook's students study fertilized chicken eggs. After they learn about the parts of a chicken egg, Terry gives each student a petri dish, a raw chicken egg, and a paper towel. The mission is to take off the outer shell but leave the rest of the egg intact inside the membrane. As the egg breaks

IDEA BANK

The samples you see on pages 45–48 show how teachers used drawings to assess students' understanding during lessons on plants, animals, and the human body. More ideas follow. Use them to inspire drawing-based assessments of your own.

Space: Design a spacesuit that would allow you to live on Mars. Label the parts of the suit and tell the purpose of each.

Five Senses: Draw a picture of something you can see (taste, touch, hear, smell).

Animals: Draw your favorite animal in a habitat that would be suitable for its survival.

Simple Machines: Draw a picture of a lever being used in your home.

Weather: Draw a picture in your weather journal of the clouds you observe in the sky each morning.

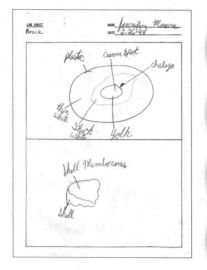

apart, students draw what they see and identify key parts that they studied earlier. Terry looks for evidence that the child observes the parts of an egg and can use science vocabulary to label them. A rubric such as the one on page 52 lets students score drawings like this.

Objective: To correctly identify and label the germ spot, chalaza, shell membrane, thick white, thin white, vitellini membrane, and yolk.

Assessment: I search for evidence that children actually drew what they saw. I can often discern this by looking at the size and location of the egg parts. I look to see that they identify and label the parts correctly. In addition to using drawing to assess content, I use the experience to assess attitude. As children are working, I circulate and notice those who are curious and encourage those who are not.

Terry Brock
Alimacani Elementary School
Jacksonville, Florida

Breaking Language Barriers

Jodene Smith uses a science book mandated by her district. Because many of her students speak English as a second language, she looks for assessment strategies that allow all of her students to express what they are learning. One way is to use the activities in the book as embedded assessments. As students participate in the activities, Jodene asks a series of questions that represent key concepts. Students can draw or write their answers. This approach lets children reflect as they are learning and bridges the communication barrier for second-language learners.

Objective: Students will correctly draw or write the answers to questions that focus on key concepts.

Assessment: Sam, an ESL student, used drawings to demonstrate understanding of some of the key concepts we studied: astronomer, day/night, eclipses. His drawings (and those of several other children) tell me that I need to reteach moon phases and the cause of moon craters.

Jodene Smith
Leal Elementary School
Cerritos, California

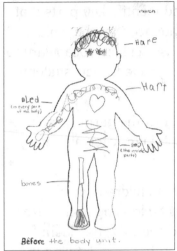

Before the body unit.

Before and After

As a pre-assessment for a unit on the human body, Debbie Weinheimer asked students in her after-school science club to sketch their "inside parts." After spending a month studying the body, she had children repeat the assignment. In individual conferences, she and her students compared the pre- and post-drawings, searching for facts and concepts that gave evidence of learning. To wrap up the unit, students used what they learned to build a life-size model of the human body, complete with internal systems.

Objective: To draw and label or explain the functions of the primary internal body systems.

Assessment: In studying Mario's pre-assessment drawing, I was able to see what he knew about the inside of the human body. I used this information to challenge Mario throughout the unit with additional questions and reading material. In his post-assessment, Mario showed an increased understanding of the internal parts of the human body. He added a brain, additional bones (ribs), and the muscular system (which he explained was attached to bones). His digestive system is more defined in the post-assessment and labeled as "intestines" rather than "guts." He also changed the shape and location of the heart and added the circulatory system. (Notice he did not connect the veins to the heart, but has blood coming out of the heart in drops. There are also drops of blood in the veins.)

Debbie Weinheimer
After School Program
Pittsburgh, Pennsylvania

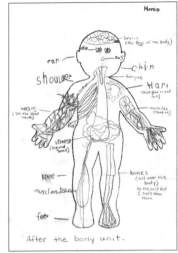

After the body unit.

TEACHING TIP

Student-Generated Rubrics

To develop a rubric for assessing drawings, I write the numbers 0 to 4 on the board and explain to children that they can earn from 0 points to 4 points on their drawings. I ask, "How would you earn 0 points?" Children usually say that if they turn in a blank piece of paper, they would earn 0 points. We work our way up from there, discussing what makes a poor drawing or an excellent drawing based on the material we've been studying. The end result is a student-generated rubric that children feel comfortable using. (See page 20 for a rubric template.)

Lynne Kepler
Clarion Limestone School
Strattranville, Pennsylvania

Evaluating Science Process Skills

First Science Drawings

Charlotte Sassman's kindergarten students are involved in a school-wide outdoor learning environment. More than a unit, this project will be part of students' learning experiences throughout their years at Carlson. Her goal is for the children to feel a sense of ownership and responsibility for the area, and then to extend that to the entire campus, neighborhood, city, state, country, and world. Charlotte begins by spending

some time exploring the area with her new students. After a few visits she challenges them to use drawings to record what they observe. She gives students science logs and a choice of drawing tools. At the beginning of the year all she looks for is something recognizable on the page. Do illustrations reflect what children observe in the environment? Charlotte also looks for evidence of organization in the

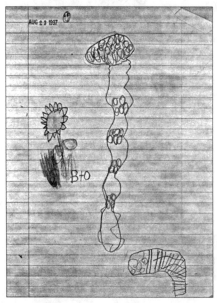

drawings, and some kind of labeling. After the first drawing assignment, Charlotte confers with each child. Children grow to believe that they *can* draw what they see, a big step in building process skills.

Objective: Students will draw what they see.

Assessment: Five-year-old Kelli has a good start on some basic process skills. "I drew it the way it looked. I tried to make it look real." Her comment also communicates her confidence as a young scientist. She has organized the information by scattering different drawings across the page to represent their placement in the outdoor learning area. She has drawn a realistic depiction of the stream bed that runs through the middle of the area, and the L-shaped ramp is in one corner. While the letters of her label— *Bto*—don't match the corresponding sounds, Kelli shows an understanding that letters go with sounds.

> *Charlotte Sassman*
> *Alice Carlson Applied Learning Center*
> *Fort Worth, Texas*

Slow Down to See

Because the world holds so much wonder for children it makes sense to focus on observation as an early science skill. This means helping them slow down to observe carefully. Ann Flagg's students observe animals in their classroom and make scientific drawings of each. When they slow down to observe, the children learn a great deal about each animal. The skills they learn through scientific drawing and careful observation will help them get more from other science experiences.

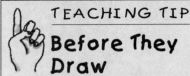

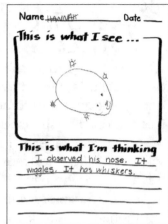

Before They Draw

When observing and drawing class pets, model the process for children first. As you observe the animal, talk about your observations as you draw. Let children see you stop to look again and again. Simply, but carefully, capture the shape of the animal and several of the details. Invite children to help you evaluate the drawing.

Before asking children to settle down and draw, let each child in a small group hold the animal (if appropriate) and talk to one another. This satisfies initial curiosity and the desire to touch and enables children to focus on drawing.

Objective: To record observations of small animals with accuracy.

Assessment: Hannah spent a great deal of time drawing in details of the hamster she observed. What does Hannah know about hamsters? She knows they have four legs and feet with claws. She knows a hamster's tail is small and thin. She represents the approximate shape and includes facial features like whiskers.

Ann Flagg
Edu-Prize School
Gilbert, Arizona

Drawing to Assess Science Attitude

Recording Observations Over Time

Lynne Kepler's third graders take turns observing the moon each night. On their assigned nights, children draw the moon as they observe it and then report their findings to the class the next day, displaying their moon drawings in sequence on a long bulletin board. Students copy the drawings into moon diaries each day to reinforce the concept that the moon's shape follows a predictable pattern.

The drawing part of this assignment allows Lynne to assess science attitudes in several ways. Students must be motivated to do the moon watch at home and return the drawings the next day. For those who love science, the drawings often inspire them to share stories of the moon watch or additional research they've done at home. Lynne's students watch the moon all year. Eventually she asks them to predict the shape of the moon. Early in the year she simply looks for an accurate representation of the moon and an enthusiasm for moon watching. You can use the assessment checklist

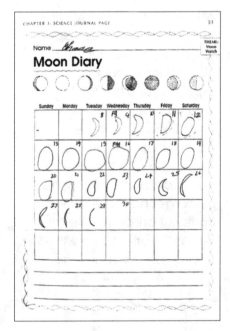

Getting Organized

Most children in my class can hardly wait for their turn at "moon homework." Even children who are not enthusiastic about drawing love this assignment. Children who normally have trouble completing homework do equally well. To help your students get the most out of an assignment like this, turn it into a family project. I prepare a "moon bag" for the moon watcher to carry home. The moon bag contains a parent letter with directions for watching the moon as well as a book about the moon that families can read together.

Lynne Kepler
Clarion Limestone School
Strattanville, Pennsylvania

on page 53 to record evidence of students' growing interests in science.

Objective: To record the phases of the moon for one month in a moon diary and conclude that the moon's shape seems to change in a pattern. To display enthusiasm about science.

Assessment: When I evaluate a moon drawing I look to see if the child captured the basic shape of the moon. On the night Chase was assigned to be the moon watcher, the moon was a waxing crescent shape. The next morning I looked to see that Chase had recorded a crescent moon and not a quarter or full moon.

Lynne Kepler
Clarion Limestone School
Strattanville, Pennsylvania

Sharing with Parents

While many parents have been admiring their children's artwork from the time the first scribbles appeared on paper, they may need guidance in understanding drawings as an assessment tool. With the ideas here, you can help parents take a fresh look at their children's drawings to gain insight about what their young scientists are learning.

◉ While it may be tempting to keep students' drawings for portfolios and parent–teacher conferences, send home a few samples to increase parents' exposure to your assessment methods. Attach the note on page 50 to help parents learn from their children's drawings. Include a copy of a student rubric if available. (See page 52.)

◉ Record the content of assessment conferences about drawings and share the information with parents. They'll appreciate your summary and feedback.

SEND-HOME SCIENCE

Name _____ Date_____

Here's what _____ 's science drawing says about _____ .

(topic)

_____

_____

_____

To find out more about your child's science learning, try asking this question:

_____

_____

SEND-HOME SCIENCE

Name _____ Date_____

Here's what _____ 's science drawing says about _____ .

(topic)

_____

_____

_____

To find out more about your child's science learning, try asking this question:

_____

_____

Rubrics, Checklists, and Other Assessments for the Science You Teach
Scholastic Professional Books, 1998

Student's Name _____ Date _____

Science Activity _____

Drawing to Enhance Observation

Customize this checklist by filling in the blanks with the subject of the student's drawing.

	EXEMPLARY	DEVELOPING	BEGINNING
Shows an interest in _____ even before it is formally introduced.			
Returns to observe _____ on a daily basis.			
Adds to the drawings in the journal without being reminded.			
Stops frequently to observe when making drawings.			
Discusses observations with other students.			
Uses science vocabulary during observation and drawing sessions.			
Demonstrates a growing curiosity by asking questions.			
Applies prior knowledge in thinking about _____ and planning drawings.			
Utilizes a variety of tools (rulers, colored pencils) in observing _____.			
Notices and records changes in _____ over time.			

Name _____ Date _____

Topic _____

My Drawing

Check the box that shows what you think of your drawing. In the box under Comments, use words to tell more about your drawing.

SCORE	CRITERIA	COMMENTS
4	**Excellent:** I try hard to draw what I see. I look up at what I am drawing to get it right. I used the drawing materials carefully and my drawing is neat.	
3	**Pretty Good:** I used some detail in my drawing. But I can see where I left out a few details.	
2	**Could Be Better:** I didn't look up at the subject while I was drawing. I missed lots of details.	
1	**Weak:** My drawing doesn't show what I observed. I didn't include details. I was not neat or careful.	

Teacher's Comments:

_____

_____

_____

Rubrics, Checklists, and Other Assessments for the Science You Teach
Scholastic Professional Books, 1998

Activity _____

Class Record: Assessing Drawings

	exemplary
✓+	exemplary
✓	proficient
✓–	needs improvement
–	not evident

NAMES	Drawings are carefully completed.	Drawings include detail, color.	Drawings include print (speech bubbles, labels, captions, and so on).	Drawings are realistic.	Drawings show positive attitude toward science.	Shows careful observation.	Shows new science understanding.	Communicates information gathered.

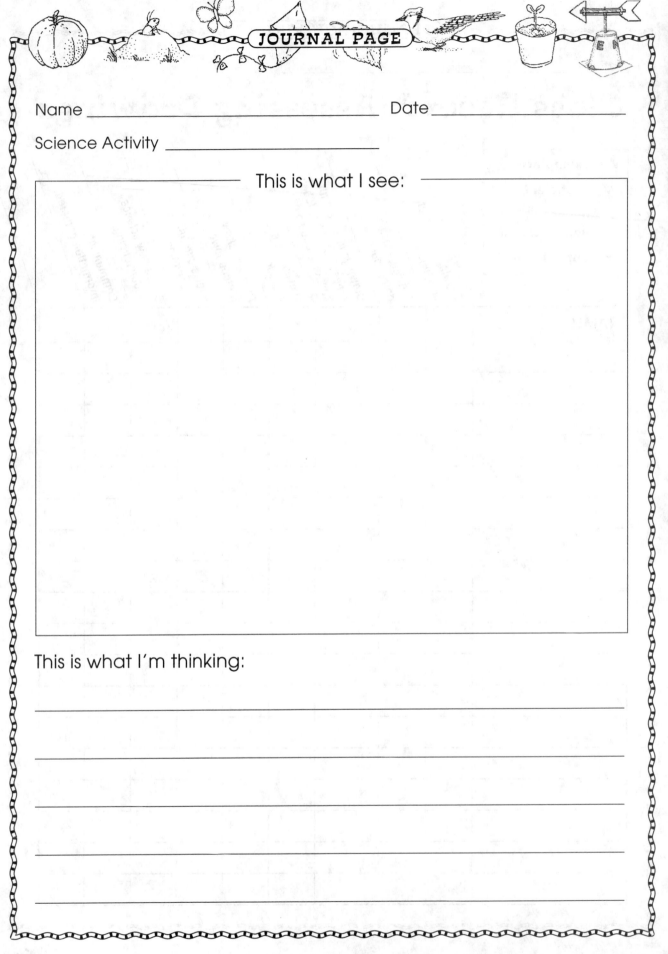

JOURNAL PAGE

Name _____ Date _____

Science Activity _____

───── This is what I see: ─────

This is what I'm thinking:

_____

_____

_____

_____

_____

Rubrics, Checklists, and Other Assessments for the Science You Teach
Scholastic Professional Books, 1998

Using Activities and Projects

A ctivities and projects let you observe children in action and assess the things that really matter: their ability to use science knowledge and skills in realistic situations and within meaningful contexts, and their attitude about the subject. As you plan activities and projects for your students, look for those that simulate real world challenges and problems. From tracking temperature and looking  for patterns, to building flying machines and discovering the principles of flight, these kinds of activities bring a sense of authenticity to the classroom and give students real reasons to learn. As your students integrate and use science knowledge during the activities you plan, you'll discover many opportunities for assessment.

Why Use Activities and Projects?

U sing activities and projects as assessment tools fits naturally with the primary science classroom. Here's how.

- Activities and projects set the stage for children to assimilate and apply new knowledge from textbooks or trade books.

- Activities and projects nurture children's multiple intelligences. For example, activities that involve designing, drawing, and building strengthen visual-spatial intelligence.

TEACHING TIP

Observation Opportunities

- Organization is the key to making time for observation. Have materials ready and accessible.

- Communicate standards of excellence, but then turn children loose. Your students will gain confidence from your trust and flexible attitude. You'll be able to spend more time actively observing.

- Products that represent significant time and effort deserve an interested audience. Be creative in finding time to share. For example, you might host a brown bag lunch in the room and invite two or three children at a time to join you each day.

Small group experiences let children stretch their interpersonal social skills.

- Interaction between children as they work can reveal science vocabulary and emerging concepts.

- Hands-on learning showcases how students apply the skills of science like measuring and observing.

- Products give evidence of following directions, and of knowledge applied in creative ways. Children have the opportunity to display thinking and problem-solving strategies that are uniquely their own.

- Misconceptions naturally emerge and are challenged as students draw on prior knowledge to make predictions. Prediction activities give a window into a child's thinking.

- Activities and products take the emphasis off reading and writing skills, areas that are still developing in young children, affording opportunity for young learners to show what they can do.

- Activities allow for flexibility in grouping. You can organize small groups, set up stations, or perform a science demonstration for the entire class. Use discussion, writing, and drawing as a follow-up to allow for individual response.

- Mid-unit activities can serve as both remediation and steering tools. Information gleaned through careful observation can be used to help students who are struggling, and to give direction for the remainder of the unit.

Looking for Learning

Products

Student products may represent hours of research and work. Other products are made in one afternoon during a science lab. Either way the end result is evidence of learning. Use these suggestions to turn products into assessment opportunities.

- Have children recall how they made the products step by step.

- Encourage children to "brag" about their work or explain to you what they are most proud of.

- Provide time for children to share products with the class.

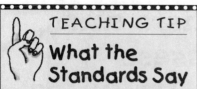
TEACHING TIP

What the Standards Say

The science standards support using activities and projects in any science program. "When students are actively engaged in assessment tasks that are similar in form to tasks in which they will engage in their lives...or are similar to the activities of scientists, great confidence can be attached to the data collected."

Record comments and answers to questions that the presenter offers.

◎ Neatness and effort really shine through in products and can represent a child's attitude towards science.

◎ Ask to see materials read or research completed in preparation for creating the product.

◎ Work together with students to write a simple rubric for scoring finished products. (See page 46.)

Activities

Children may participate in numerous science activities each week. Keeping records over time can reveal trends or patterns that may be overlooked in short term observations.

◎ Set up a notebook tabbed with each child's name or make an index card for each child. Record questions and explanations offered, observed behaviors and insights, as well as problems encountered.

◎ Body language can reveal attitudes about science. Is the child leaning forward, actively manipulating materials, offering ideas and suggestions?

◎ Turn expectations into questions to ask yourself as you observe the students: Who is a keen observer? Who has creatively found a way to solve the problem? Who is measuring accurately? Who is recording data?

◎ Be alert for demonstrations of creative thinking that exceed your expectations. Observation can reveal insights into advanced inquiry skills or emerging science concepts.

◎ Stop and ask questions as children work. For example: What would happen if_____?

How is the material reacting? How would you explain what you see? To help students improve, announce positive science behaviors as you observe them. "I like the way Josh is using the hand lens to study the back of the leaf."

◎ Revisit an activity and watch for growth over time. Given the same activity, how do inquiry skills improve over the course of the year?

Using Checklists and Rubrics to Assess Projects and Activities

Checklists and rubrics can help organize your assessment of projects and activities and provide evidence of learning both during the process and over time. Using the information on page 9 as a guide, work with students to write a simple rubric for scoring finished products. (See Teaching Tip, page 46.) What will an "excellent" project or activity look like? How will they know if they could to try harder next time? Sharing this information at the beginning with students helps them set goals for themselves. Use the checklists on pages 64–68 as they appear or as models for customizing your own. Include detailed information on what you're looking for in terms of content, skills, and attitude. For group work, use the form on page 68 to let students reflect on the experience. Reproducible process skills checklists including "Assessing Model-Making Skills" (page 19) will support assessment of projects and activities.

Assessment in Action

The following samples offer an inside look at some of the ways teachers are using projects and activities to assess growth in content, process skills, and attitude. Practical tips for managing assessment appear in the margins. Reproducible checklists and rubrics appear at the end of this section. You can use them as is, or customize them to better meet your needs.

Activities and Projects to Evaluate Content

Making Models

On a recent field trip to a nature reserve, Dee Wenner's students observed a beaver dam. The children were highly interested, so when they returned to the classroom their teacher gathered up books and other resources to learn more. As a take-home assignment, students constructed beaver dam models that would represent the purpose and structure of a dam. Proud of the results, Dee's students displayed the models at open house as an example of their science learning.

Objective: To construct a beaver dam that shows materials

IDEA BANK

The samples on pages 58–62 show how teachers use activities and products to assess student understanding during lessons on bulbs, bones, measuring, and more. Additional activity and project ideas follow.

Magnets: Design a game using magnets and explain it to others.

Matter: Describe the properties of snow as it changes from one state to another.

Sound: Experiment with glasses filled with different amounts of colored water.

Simple Machines: Use a pulley to design a machine that makes one classroom routine easier.

Weather: Construct a wind catcher and use it to monitor the direction of the wind.

that beavers use and the effects of a beaver dam on the environment.

Assessment: I was looking for evidence in the models that the children understood two concepts: Dams change the environment by changing water patterns, and beavers use natural and readily available materials like branches and small stones to build. Each child was required to present his or her model to the class and explain what  it demonstrated. As the children spoke, I gave points for each beaver fact mentioned. I also gave points for creativity and effort that showed a positive attitude about science learning.

> Dee Wenner
> Immaculate Conception School
> Clarion, Pennsylvania

Activities in Art

Art projects combine children's natural curiosity for the world with their innate creativity. In Linda Hancock's class, students sponge-painted skeletons after studying the human body. They looked at real bones, pictures of bones, and x-rays of bones; then Linda Hancock's students were ready to sponge paint their own skeletons to demonstrate what they had learned. The children were given a variety of sponge shapes to use with white paint to create a skeleton.

Objective: To represent the major bones of the body in a sponge painting.

Assessment: Sara's picture shows that she has a good grasp of how the body is  put together. She follows the progression from head to toe but has left out or added interesting details. Her picture includes toes but not fingers, and hips but not ribs. She depicts the spine as many separate bones that are connected. Her arms show that she understands the concept of joints.

Linda Hancock
CMU Children's School
Pittsburgh, Pennsylvania

Evaluating Science Process Skills

Communicating Information

An important part of any scientist's job is to communicate findings to others. One way Rita Devlin helps develop this skill in her students is to set up situations in which one group of children has information that needs to be shared with the rest of the class. For example, she worked with one group to make paper from sawdust and materials from nature. After they completed the process, this group had to "teach" the process to the rest of the class.

Objective: Students will work as a team to make paper, record the procedure, and communicate it to others.

Assessment: After the first group made paper, they talked over the steps, recorded them on chart paper, then presented the process to the class. They were confident in their communication to the class and cooperated to present the material. Communicating with others is important in this activity because the rest of the class will go on to make paper based on the description given by the first group. Setting up this real-life need for communication helps children realize how important it is to communicate with accuracy.

Rita Devlin
CMU Children's School
Pittsburgh, Pennsylvania

Prediction and Observation

Charlotte Sassman purchased an amaryllis bulb packaged in a box with a pot. Before her students opened the box, she asked them to predict what would be inside. Since there was a picture of a large red amaryllis bloom on the box, many responses related to that. "I think it is a flower because the picture

Book Link

Papermaking for Kids by Beth Wilkinson (Gibbs-Smith, 1997) contains basic how-tos for papermaking, plus fun ideas for getting fancy.

shows it." Students stretched out the letters on the box, "a-m-a-r-y-l-l-i-s b-u-l-b," and talked about what kind of bulb this could be ("like a light bulb?"), then took it out, put it in the pot, and watched it grow. Along the way they recorded observations in their journals.

Objective: Students will grow in their observation and recording skills.

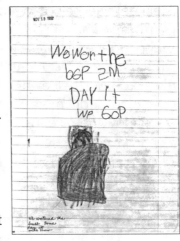

Assessment: After replanting, we discussed how a scientist would observe and draw exactly what he or she sees. We closely examined the bulb, noting the colors, shape of the stem and bulb, relative size of bulb and pot, etc. Then the children moved to independently record what they had observed. After completing a couple of observations, we made a rubric for journal observations with a happy/sad face format that is easy for everyone to use. In this sample I can tell that Lauren's confidence as an observer has grown. By comparing the size of the print and choice of writing instruments (to earlier journal entries) I can see how her writing skills are maturing.

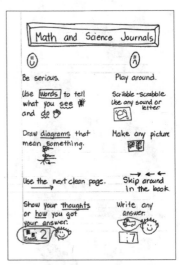

Charlotte Sassman
Alice Carlson Applied
Learning Center
Fort Worth, Texas

Measuring, Comparing, and Collecting Data

Bob Krech's students explore the concepts of balance and weight through guided hands-on experiences that begin with balancing paper butterflies on a pencil eraser and include making mobiles and working with simple beam balances and equal bucket balances. Unifix cubes are used when appropriate as a standardized measure for weight. A favorite culminating activity has students using all that they have learned to determine which of five sealed canisters contain six marbles.

Objective: Students will apply a strategy based on previous experience with weighing and balancing to discover which of five sealed film canisters contains six marbles.

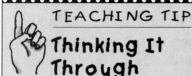
Assessment: This activity is simple to assess but also provides a way for me to gather much information about my students. The children are so engrossed in this activity that I am free to circulate among them and ask questions to determine what they are thinking. Examples of comments include, "You can hear how many marbles are inside by shaking it." "You've got to count the container. It weighs something." I record comments and use them to assess each child's understanding. Students beam with satisfaction when they solve the mystery because they are using science and math skills that they have learned.

Bob Krech
Dutch Neck School
Princeton Junction, New Jersey

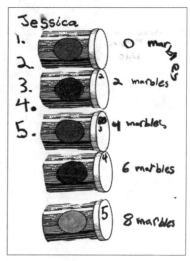

Balancing and Weighing, from the National Science Resource Center (See page 10)

Evaluating Attitude

Games Bring out Science Attitudes

As a part of a unit on animals in their environment, Dee Wenner's students study the concept of camouflage. To assess understanding and attitude, she has children camouflage a potato to survive in a forested area by their school grounds. Children spend considerable time studying the area and then decorating the potato so that it will be hidden by the environment.

Objective: To demonstrate understanding of camouflage by carefully camouflaging a potato so that it can remain hidden in a natural environment.

Assessment: I was looking for evidence that the child understood the concept of camouflage, as shown by using materials that matched the environment. After the potatoes were found, children explained the finer points of their camouflage design to classmates. It was at this point that enthusiasm and interest really showed in some students. I made notes on interest and effort during this activity.

Dee Wenner
Immaculate Conception School
Clarion, Pennsylvania

Date _____

Exploring Science at Home

Floating boats in the bathtub, planting a garden, blowing soap bubbles, or baking a batch of cookies: Early science skills begin at home. Just as reading with your child enhances school performance, exploring the world around you builds science understanding. You can encourage your child's interest in science with everyday activities. Here are some suggestions.

Sort It Out: Junk drawers are a perfect way to strengthen important science skills such as classifying and organizing. Pull one out, check for unsafe objects, and let your child sort it all out. Along the way, encourage your child to share reasons for sorting choices.

In the Kitchen: Cooking projects are one way to show the science that happens around us every day. Invite your child to help prepare simple foods. Look for changes in the ingredients together. If you're adventurous, give your child an assortment of ingredients such as baking soda, water, cornstarch, food coloring, and so on. Let your child mix them at will to see what happens.

Card Constructors: When you're done playing Go Fish, use the cards to build a tower. How high can you go? What makes the best base? Try stacking other materials, too: bathroom tissue tubes, plastic cups, and other odds and ends.

Student's Name _____ Date _____

Activity _____

10 Things to Look For
During Hands-on Science Activities

ASSESSMENT AREA	CHECK	COMMENTS
1. Shows curiosity about the science topic.		
2. Gives reasoning for predictions.		
3. Predictions get more accurate over time.		
4. Follows activity steps.		
5. Uses standard and non-standard measuring tools to gather information.		
6. Uses detail in drawings.		
7. Writing and discussion shows grasp of science vocabulary.		
8. Exchanges information with others.		
9. Works cooperatively with a group.		
10. Shows understanding of key concepts.		

Rubrics, Checklists, and Other Assessments for the Science You Teach
Scholastic Professional Books, 1998

Student's Name _____ Date _____

Activity/Project _____

Assessing Activities and Projects

SCORE	CRITERIA	COMMENTS
4	**Full Accomplishment** Student correctly performs the activity. Student is able to observe and record all changes occurring during the activity.	
3	**Substantial Accomplishment** Student correctly performs the activity. Student is able to observe and record most of the changes occurring during the activity.	
2	**Partial Accomplishment** Student correctly performs the activity but needs help to do it. Student is able to observe and record some of the changes occurring during the activity.	
1	**Little or No Accomplishment** Student misunderstands the task or makes little or no effort to perform the activity.	

Name _____ Date _____

I made a model of _____

My Model

Read the description for each score. Which one best describes your model?

SCORE	CRITERIA	WHAT I WANT YOU TO KNOW
3	I looked carefully at the real thing (or a picture of it). I looked again as I was making my model. I used lots of details in my model. I can name at least three ways my model is like the real thing.	
2	I looked at the real thing (or pictures) before I made my model but I didn't look again. I used some details in my model. My model shows some of what I learned but I left some things out. My model looks kind of like the real thing. I can see ways I could make my model look more like the real thing.	
1	I didn't look at the real thing (or pictures) to make my model. My model doesn't show details. My model doesn't look much like the real thing. I didn't try to show what I learned in my model.	

Rubrics, Checklists, and Other Assessments for the Science You Teach
Scholastic Professional Books, 1998

Name _____ Date _____

Activitiy or Project _____

What Did I Learn?

Draw a face to show
how you feel about
the project or activity.
Then answer the questions.

1. One problem I had was _____

   _____

2. One thing I did well was _____

   _____

3. Advice I would give to another student about this activity
   or project is

   _____

4. An idea I would like to learn more about is _____

   _____

5. Something else I would like you to know is _____

   _____

On the back of this paper, use pictures or words to tell about
something you learned.

Name _____ Date _____

Activitiy or Project _____

We Work Together

1. Color in the face that shows how you feel about each statement.

I know my group job.

I ask questions.

I share materials and ideas.

I can ask for help.

I wait for my turn.

I check my work.

2. In my group I did:

_____ all of the work   _____ most of the work   _____ a fair amount of the work

3. One thing our group is good at is_____

_____

4. Something our group can do better next time is _____

_____

_____

Using Conversations for Assessment

The ability to understand what a child is saying is the essence of assessment. Since verbal skills often surpass writing and drawing abilities in the early years, weaving opportunities for verbal demonstrations of science skills into your assessment plan is essential. Using science conversations for assessment involves listening, observing, asking questions, and listening again. The process is continuous and active, and is as natural to the classrooms of young children as building with blocks.

Keep in mind that children who are accustomed to taking multiple choice, textbook-style science quizzes may have trouble answering questions that begin with words like compare, explain, describe, or what if… Spend some instructional time modeling how to answer these questions. With training and patience, children's comfort levels will increase and so will the quality of their responses.

Why Conversations Work?

Whether you're talking with one student or the whole class, keep these tips in mind to encourage conversations full of insight and information.

- Make group discussion time a safe time. Children must be free to comment without fear of ridicule. Allow plenty of "think time" as well, to give each student time to respond without interruption.

- Focus conversations by defining your purpose and objectives for the discussion.

- Keep opening questions simple and direct. Start with a simple question that leads to only one answer, to get the ball rolling. Once children feel successful, ask open-ended questions that get students to think creatively and critically.

- Conference together to critique a work sample using pre-

TEACHING TIP

Many Voices

Give children opportunities to demonstrate learning through conferences, presentations, conversations, class brainstorming sessions, dramatics, and other verbally-based activities. Students will shine when given an assortment of "voices" to demonstrate what they know.

established criteria. Rubrics and checklists make it easy to stay on track.

◙ Watch for quiet children who have much to share but lack confidence to speak up in a group. Gathering small groups together to discuss probing questions related to a unit gives children a safe place to reveal their own thinking. In the process of listening to one another, they'll expand their own ideas and accept new ways of thinking. Make note of children's ideas and insights.

◙ As children work with science materials in cooperative groups, interview children to capture verbal snapshots of learning in progress. Keep a checklist handy to record assessment information. (See page 77.)

◙ Make time for conversations with individual students. In addition to trying to meet with a few students a day while they work, you might invite one child each day to walk with you during recess duty. Students look forward to these special times, and will often open up and share their unique perspective.

◙ Don't let silence kill a discussion. Children need a few moments to think before answering a challenging question, but then may be reluctant to be the first to break the long silence brought about by wait time. To avoid awkward silence, fill the space with a light, focused comment as you wait for children to respond. In other words, ask a question, comment, ask the question again, and then look for a response.

◙ Ask one student to paraphrase or explain what another student has said. Or piggyback questions; have students comment on or add to a classmate's response.

◙ Probe deeper for insights and help students learn to defend their answers with questions like these:

  Can you explain that further?

  Did you consider _____?

  What have we learned in science class that causes you to believe that?

  Is there another way of thinking about that?

TEACHING TIP

Many Voices

Julia and Marti got a close look at a sunflower plant, and I got a chance to do some informal assessment while we talked. Since there were no other sunflowers nearby, the girls wanted to know how the sunflower came to grow. "I'm not sure," I answered. "How could a seed from a sunflower get here and grow? I know there are giant sunflowers planted in the garden behind the school." After a little discussion, Marti decided that "a bird was eating the seeds and dropped one here in the flower bed." Julia said, "One of them was trying to eat too many (seeds) and couldn't fly with all of them in his mouth, so it fell out. Right here!"

Charlotte Sassman
Alice Carlson Applied
Learning Center
Fort Worth, Texas

TEACHING TIP

KWL Charts

To start a lesson with an information-filled conversation, try using a modified KWL chart (What I Know, What I Want to Know, What I Learned). After asking children what they know, immerse students in the topic through books, materials, and so on. Follow up by asking students what they'd like to know (K). Their questions will be richer after this immersion period. Add a fourth column (What's Next?) to the traditional chart to let children know that learning is never complete and questions seldom exhausted.

Book Link

For excellent samples of science conversations between children and teachers, read *Doing What Scientists Do* by Ellen Dorris (Heinemann, 1991).

Using Checklists and Rubrics to Assess Conversations

An all-purpose class checklist, like the one Pat Sylvan uses (see page 77), comes in handy when you want to record students' participation in discussions. You'll be able to tell a lot from this checklist: who's talking, who you need to draw out, what direction students take in their conversations, the interests they show, and so on. The conversation record sheet on page 79 and student rubric on page 80 will also help you assess conversations. Remember to incorporate the process skills checklists on pages 11–20, as you listen in on your students.

Opening Doors to Discussions

Use comments and questions like these to help draw students out during individual interviews:

Describe your project to me.

What did you learn through the activity?

What did you already know that helped you understand our investigation?

What surprised you the most about the experiment we did today?

Is there a problem I could help you to solve?

What do you think might happen next?

Have you read any books about this topic?

If I changed XX about the investigation what do you think would happen?

How did you decide to solve the problem that way?

How have your original ideas changed?

Was this experiment difficult for you? How?

If you could change one part of our investigation what would it be?

What would you like to learn next about this topic?

IDEA BANK

The samples you see on pages 72–77 show how teachers use science conversations to assess students' growth during lessons on plants, the moon, paper-making, and more. Additional suggestions for using conversations follow.

◎ Let students interview one another on science topics, with one child playing the part of a reporter, the other the part of "scientist."

◎ Produce narrated film clips on science topics.

◎ Audio tape science discussions. Play the tapes back for students, charting steps, main points, or questions.

◎ Set aside time at open school night for parents to ask their young scientists about science activities in progress. Informative conversations will ensue.

Assessment in Action

The following examples offer an inside look at some of the ways teachers are using drama, concept maps, group discussions, conferencing, and other verbally-based techniques to assess content, process skills, and attitude. Examples of children's work are followed by comments from their classroom teachers. You can adapt both to work with other science lessons you teach. Practical tips for managing hands-on assessment appear in the margins.

Evaluating Content

Conversations and Concept Maps

Before beginning a new unit Ann Flagg often works with the class to construct a concept map. A concept map diagrams the relationship between key concepts related to a topic. The map provides a picture of student misconceptions and pinpoints areas where the children need information and experiences. She can also see at a glance what most already know, so that they can build on prior knowledge and go on from there. The example here is from a unit on the moon. At the end of the unit she gave students a list of moon words. They used them to build a concept map, taking time for related conversations along the way.

Objective: To determine misconceptions and prior knowledge about the moon.

Assessment: From the map, you can see that our conversation about the moon revealed that most

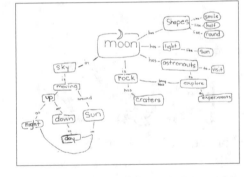

children in the class come to the moon unit with an awareness that the moon appears to change. However, students did not demonstrate an awareness of why these changes occur (nor would this be expected at this age). They know the moon is made of rock and that it moves in the sky, but some stated that it moves around the sun rather than rotates around the Earth. Students are aware that the moon gives off light, but several stated that it was like the sun.

Ann Flagg
Edu-Prize School
Gilbert, Arizona

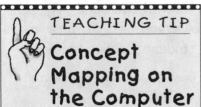
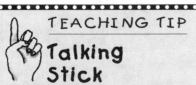
Stage a Show

As part of a unit on animals, Ann Flagg's first-grade class studied plant-eating and meat-eating animals. Toward the end of the unit they studied animals that are extinct. The children were anxious to learn about dinosaurs, so they looked at herbivores and carnivores. As a post-assessment activity the children formed small groups, made dinosaur masks, and developed dinosaur dramas. Ann asked that they include the eating habits of both an herbivore and a carnivore dinosaur in their productions. As you might expect, many of the children chose to show Tyrannosaurus Rex attacking a plant-eating dinosaur.

Objective: Create and perform a drama that shows the eating preferences of both a carnivorous and herbivorous dinosaur.

Assessment: The first group's show began with a plant-eating dinosaur walking in a lake and peacefully eating the plants from the bottom of the pond. Another plant-eater was grazing on low-hanging trees. A meat-eater arrived on the scene and attempted to eat the dinosaur in the water, but ended up feasting on the other dinosaur. The children showed through actions and words that dinosaurs can be both carnivorous and herbivorous.

Ann Flagg
Edu-Prize School
Gilbert, Arizona

Conversations With Guests

Our school celebrates Grandparents' and Special Friends' Day in the fall. Each child can invite one adult to come to school. One of the centers on this day was a "Skeleton Quiz." On the table with the quiz were books about bones. Children worked with their guests to answer the questions on this quiz. Conversations naturally

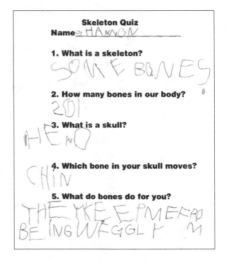

73

occurred as students and their guests worked to find out answers. After the quizzes were collected I used the answers as a pre-assessment to find out what students needed to know.

Objective: Work with a special guest and use resource materials to find answers to the Skeleton Quiz.

Assessment: I observed that Sharon and her guest were involved in an active conversation about bones. Sharon was able to use resource materials, including her guest, to answer questions. Sharon's quiz also showed that I need to focus some teaching on the skull as well as help Sharon understand that bones are a living part of the body.

Ann Flagg
Edu-Prize School
Gilbert, Arizona

Evaluating Science Process Skills

Tell Me About It

For one week the children in Wendy Weiner's class worked with the concept of balances. They used balance scales and played with toys that balance. At the end of the unit, she asked the class to demonstrate, through a drawing, that they understand the concept of balance. Wendy conferenced with each child so that he or she could add explanation to the drawing, and recorded each child's explanation directly on the test paper.

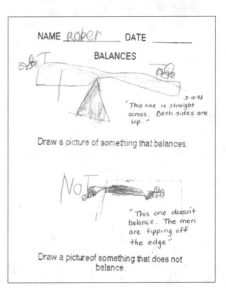

Objective: Students will show that they understand the concept of balance in a drawing and communicate an explanation of their drawing in a conference.

Assessment: Robert demonstrated an understanding of the concept of balance in both his drawing and the follow-up conference. He was having trouble drawing and explaining his picture of something that does not balance. Nevertheless, when I got out the scale and asked him to show an example of something that did not balance, he was able to do so.

Wendy Weiner
Bryant Elementary School
Milwaukee, Wisconsin

Teachable Moments in Conversations

As part of the project approach to learning, Charlotte Sassman looks for ways to work objectives into meaningful activities. For a unit on plants, she wanted the children to learn the names of the parts of a plant, and to compare a flower and a weed. By doing a comparison, she hoped students would discover that all plants share common characteristics (roots, stem, leaf, and flower). To accomplish this, she and her students observed a school flower bed. A wonderful conversation flowed as they tried to name each plant. Out of this conversation, children began to compare flowers and weeds. After close observation, they discovered that both flowers and weeds have roots, stems, leaves, and flowers.

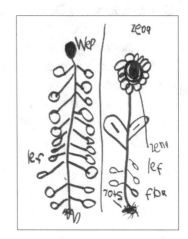

Objective: Children will utilize observation skills to identify and compare the parts of a plant and the parts of a weed. Children recorded information from the conversation in their science journals.

Assessment: Amanda's drawing shows that she recognized common characteristics of a zinnia and a weed. In addition to observing Amanda during the writing, I conferenced with her to draw out more information. She told me about the roots that hold up the plant. In the course of our conversation I learned more about what she knew, and Amanda was able to set some goals for later journal entries.

Charlotte Sassman
Alice Carlson Applied Learning Center
Fort Worth, Texas

Why Didn't It Work?

"Do plants need soil to grow?" As a part of a unit on plants, Kelly Freeman's students worked in groups to answer this question. To test the prediction, "Plants do not need soil to grow," the children planted grass seeds on natural sponges, but the seeds did not grow. In order to understand what the children were thinking, Kelly conferenced with each group. They considered the variables of the experiment, and decided that one of the reasons the seeds did not grow is that the seeds did not get enough water. The children knew that they had to provide water for growth and decided to try the investigation again using a different kind of sponge.

Objective: Develop an understanding of making predictions. Work with variables to design an effective investigation to test the prediction.

Assessment: I recorded conversations with students and used them to evaluate their emerging understanding of the scientific method and their ability to eliminate variables to solve problems.

Teacher: Why do you think the grass did not grow on the natural sponges?

Alyssa: All the light was taking up the water.

Audrey: I gave it too much water.

Teacher: The thing is, though, every time I came in and looked at the sponge, it was dry. Alyssa says the light took up the water. How did it take up the water?

Devyn: It evaporated it.

Teacher: If the water evaporated, what happened to the seeds?

Audrey: It took up the seeds with it?

Teacher: Well, are the seeds still there?

(Children look at sponge.)

Devyn: It dried up the seeds, but the seeds are still there.

Teacher: So the seeds just didn't have a chance to grow? Was it because there was no soil, or because they did not have enough water?

Devyn: Some seeds have to wait thousands of years and then they can grow.

Teacher: How could we find the answer to the question of why they did not grow?

Audrey: We have to make sure they have enough water to know for sure.

Teacher: Yes, we could still grow the same grass seeds, but we need to let them have more water. So, let's try the experiment again using a different kind of sponge that will hold more water. (Shows synthetic sponge.) Do you think the seeds will grow this time?

Devyn: Yeah, I think they will grow a tiny bit.

Teacher: Do you have any more predictions?

Alyssa: I do. I think that the more we water them, the more they will grow.

Teacher: Anyone else?

Devyn: Some plants need a lot of water, like grass plants. Other kinds of plants like cactus don't need much water. I think we need to water the grass a little more than a regular plant.

Kelly Freeman
Edu-Prize School
Gilbert, Arizona

TEACHING TIP

Class List on a Clipboard

I always keep a clipboard on my desk with a class list, so that when I'm questioning or leading a discussion I can quickly give my students a √+, √, √- to evaluate their responses. I use a wider grid when I want to write specific observation—for example, during hands-on experiments and activities.

Pat Sylvan
Pine Grove Elementary School
Simsbury, Connecticut

Assessing Attitude

Discovery Table Talk

Rita Devlin and Linda Hancock involve parents in science conversations with their children at a "discovery table." This is a place where children and families get together to share topics of interest. Together, they plan a presentation. They transcribe each child's comments for assessment purposes, but the most important part is that the child takes an enthusiastic role in the process.

This is my raccoon skeleton. I used it for my Discovery Table. We found it in our woods. My Dad saw a raccoon die and he remembered it.
A week before my Discovery Table we dug it up. Some of the fur was on it, so we had to dig some dirt with the fur.
We put the bones in the case. We tried to fit the body together. First we put some sand and dirt in the box.
My Discovery Table was about bones.
A Paleontologist digs up bones.
Some of those bones may be dinosaur bones. They look a lot like a baby egg stealer.

BRENDAN

Objective: Student will communicate with enthusiasm about a topic of interest.

Children will show enthusiasm by planning the unit with a parent, gathering the materials, and following up the presentation with a report.

Assessment: Brendan came to class well prepared and bubbling with excitement. He told the story of finding the skeleton in the woods and digging it up just for the discovery table. It was obvious from his description that Brendan was involved in the process of preparing the bones for display. His use of the word "paleontologist" shows that he and his parents did some additional research.

Rita Devlin and Linda Hancock
CMU Children's School
Pittsburgh, Pennsylvania

Sharing With Parents

Wth conversation as the goal, invite students to attend your next parent/teacher conference. Child-driven conferences can be affirming, and hold a child accountable in a positive way. If students keep science portfolios, use these as a springboard for child-driven conversation. For information on what students might include in their portfolios, see page 11. A form on which you record questions and responses during conversations with students will also be a useful tool for sharing with parents. (See page 79.)

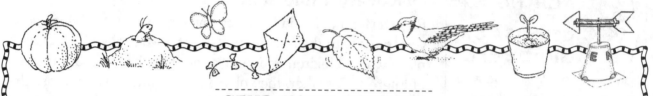

SEND-HOME SCIENCE

Dear Families,

Young children are often able to verbally communicate what they know much more easily than by other methods, such as writing and drawing. Many of the everyday activities you do with your child at home can be informal science investigations: pouring bath water, building with blocks, tending the garden, cooking, and feeding birds are just a few examples. To draw out your child's scientific thinking, try these conversations starters:

As your child observes something ask:

  ▣ What is happening? Tell me more.

  ▣ How does it feel? (taste, look, sound, etc.)

If your child has a question, answer it with another question.

  ▣ Good question! How can we find out?

  ▣ What are your ideas?

Rubrics, Checklists, and Other Assessments for the Science You Teach
Scholastic Professional Books, 1998

Name _____   Date _____

Topic _____

Our Science Conversation

TEACHER'S QUESTIONS	STUDENT'S RESPONSES	COMMENTS
1.		
2.		
3.		
4.		
5.		
6.		
7.		
8.		

Name _____ Date _____

Title of Presentation_____

My Presentation

Circle the score that describes your presentation. In the box under Comments, use words to tell more about your presentation.

SCORE	CRITERIA	COMMENTS
3	I spoke so all could hear. My presentation represented at least 3 new concepts I learned in this unit. I included several visual aids or props	
2	Most of the time I spoke so all could hear. My presentation represented at least 2 new concepts I learned in this activity. I included one visual aid or prop.	
1	It was difficult to hear my presentation. My presentation did not include new concepts. I did not include a visual aid or prop.	

Teacher's Comments:

_____

_____

_____

Rubrics, Checklists, and Other Assessments for the Science You Teach
Scholastic Professional Books. 1998